T ST

LAN

ONI MITCHELL ANTHONY KIEDIS

SSETTE CARLY SIMON BONNIE

ORI AMOS BRUCE SPRINGSTEEN

ERIC CLAPTON SINÉAD O'CONNOR

ND KEITH RICHARDS JOHNNY

IDERSON COURTNEY LOVE STING

ET JACKSON LISA STANSFIELD

AVID BOWIE k. d. lang ELTON JOHN

THE

Rolling Stone

BOOK *of* LOVE

THE

RollingSto

BOOK of LOVE

Rolling Stone Press

Compiled by the editors of

RUNNING PRESS

PHILADELPHIA · LONDON

very phrase "rock & roll" was originally a euphemism for sex and love has been contemporary songwriters' most popular topic, it would seem musicians have a lot to say on the subject.

And indeed they do. Here, we've compiled the most scintillating, amusing, moving and whimsical quotes musicians have uttered on the subject in the pages of ROLLING STONE.

The Editors
Rolling Stone Press

ALL WE NEED I

I BELIEVE I

IT'S DAMN HA

BUT I ABSOLU'

BELIEVE I

John Lennon
ISSUE 73 · January 7th,

IT'S A SHAME PEOPLE HAVE THIS REALLY WEIRD CONCEPTION OF WHAT LOVE IS AND WHAT HATE IS LOVE AND HATE ARE THE SAME THING. BOY GEORGE

ISSUE 423 JUNE 7TH, 1982

Love is **two** minutes and **fifty** seconds of **squelching** noises.

Johnny Rotten,

(a.k.a. John Lydon)

ISSUE 250 · October 20th, 1977

unno what
eally, and
it doesn't
EXIST in
my songs.

I would have loved to grow up in a place where they tell you, "You make me crazy. I love you, I love you," that sort of thing.

Melissa Etheridge

ISSUE 698/699 · December 29th, 1994·
January 12th, 1995

When you fall in love, you feel like a missing piece of a puzzle that's been found.

David Byrne

ISSUE 524 · April 21st, 1988

When a man's looking for a woman, he ain't looking for a woman who's an airplane pilot. He's looking for a woman to help him out

angerous as hell being this in
time. The idea of danger

and support him, to
hold up one end while
he holds up another.

BOB DYLAN

ISSUE 278 • November 16th, 1978

You have faith and hope and love
as a child and lose them very early.
You spend your whole life with
just fragments of them left.

Joni Mitchell
ISSUE 383 · November 25th, 1982

Being in love was not **the m**
important thing to me; be
respected was

Tori Amos

ISSUE 685 · June 30th, 1994

It's a

love all the

has never been clearer to me.

Kristin Hersh

(Throwing Muses)

ISSUE 703 · March 9th, 1995

I have so

love

David Bowie
(referring to wife Iman)
ISSUE 648 · January 21st, 1993

itr

meone who

s me for me.

Seriously,

eally helps.

[Love is] . . . that basic need that's inside of you to just bury your head in someone's armpit.

Neneh Cherry

ISSUE 649 · February 4th, 1993

When I gave birth to my daughter and they put her in my arms, I thought: "This has got to be it. . . . This is the ultimate." I haven't experienced anything greater.

Whitney Houston

ISSUE 658 · June 10th, 1993

SO WHAT IS LOVE? P.31

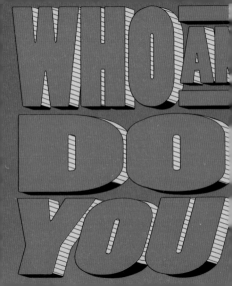

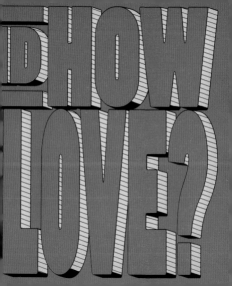

Like so many MILLIONS OF LOVE WOMEN. I love their THINK and the way THEY T and the way THEY FEEL. I d Yes, I have a STRONG APP THAT DOESN'T MEAN I'm KIEDIS (Red Hot Chili Peppe

OTHER MEN on this planet,

essence and the way THEY

LK and the way THEY MOVE

n't think it's terribly unusual.

ECIATION for women. But

a WOMANIZER. ANTHONY

s) ISSUE 679 · April 7th, 1994

WHO AND HOW DO YOU LOVE? #25

I'm very much into adrenaline, really. I like to pursue flights of fancy, then I get bored with them and have a few hours of indifference until another mad passion grabs me.

Thomas Dolby

ISSUE 394 · April 2th8, 1983

Every time I fall in love, I'm hope-lessly in love. I would kill anybody who tried to take away what's mine. But I wouldn't put myself into a relationship unless it were really special. Because I'm number one now, I have to be very careful.

Boy George

ISSUE 423 · June 7th, 1984

STING ISSUE 457 • SEPTEMBER 26TH, 1985

THE NIGHT MY LITTLE BOY WAS BORN, IT WAS AMAZING. I'VE PLAYED ONSTAGE FOR HUNDREDS OF THOUSANDS OF PEOPLE, AND I'VE FELT MY OWN SPIRIT REALLY RISE SOME NIGHTS. BUT WHEN HE CAME OUT, I HAD THIS FEEL-

BRUCE SPRINGSTEEN

FOR GIVING ME THAT SENSE OF FUTURE HISTORY!

ING OF A KIND OF LOVE THAT I HADN'T EXPERIENCED BE-FORE. AND THE MINUTE I FELT IT, IT WAS TERRIFYING. . . . BUT IT'S ALSO A WINDOW INTO ANOTHER WORLD. AND IT'S THE WORLD THAT I WANT TO LIVE IN RIGHT NOW.

ISSUE 468 · AUGUST 6TH, 1992

ACTUALLY CARE WHAT THE WORLD'S GOING

With [Lou Reed], a lot of dynamics
that I really hadn't seen come into
focus. It's like what happens when
two people who can't stop talking
start talking; we just kinda haven't
stopped.

Laurie Anderson

ISSUE 706 · April 20th, 1995

My love for Carly [Simon] is a very religious thing, to me, because sometimes I just exchange with her completely and I don't know where I end off and she begins.

James Taylor

ISSUE 125 · January 4th, 1973

I have this real obsession with grace. That's the number one thing I look for in a person in the physiological realm.

Courtney Love

(Hole)
ISSUE 697 · December 15th, 1994

When you love, you love. I mean, do you stop loving somebody because you have different images?

Whitney Houston

ISSUE 658 · June 10th, 1993

I don't want to be a swinger. Like I said in the song, I've been through it all, and nothing works better than to have somebody you love hold you.

JOHN LENNON
ISSUE 73 · January 7th, 1971

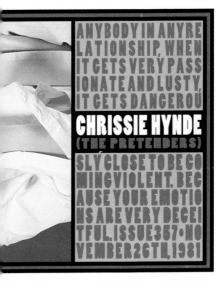

ANYBODY IN ANY RELATIONSHIP, WHEN IT GETS VERY PASSIONATE AND LUSTY, IT GETS DANGEROU

CHRISSIE HYNDE
(THE PRETENDERS)

SLY CLOSE TO BECOMING VIOLENT. BECAUSE YOUR EMOTIONS ARE VERY DECEITFUL. ISSUE 357 • NOVEMBER 26TH, 1981

Being a good father is pretty much my number one concern in life.

Flea (Red Hot Chili Peppers)

ISSUE 719 · October 19th, 1995

Family. . . . It's one of the most special things that you'll ever get on the face of this earth. It gives you that final missing link of what life's about. While they're looking upon you as the most wonderful person in the world because you're "Daddy," they do more for you than you do for them.

Keith Richards

(the Rolling Stones)
ISSUE 536 · October 6th, 1988

I love a pupil-teacher relationship. Basically, I want somebody who makes me laugh. I want to giggle my way into oblivion. I want my partner to be on the same wavelength; I couldn't sleep with someone who wasn't funny.

Bette Midler

ISSUE 384 · December 9th, 1982

I wasn't the best husband. We had a good thing, and I don't think I was really ready to be married. I thought I was, made a mistake and wasn't. But once that was over, oddly enough, I didn't want to go out on dates. I didn't want to go out and pretend I was nineteen again.

Paul Westerberg

ISSUE 659 · June 24th, 1993

I once said I'd never have a

lover who ate meat. I sort of

laid that down as the law. And

I remember sitting across the

table from this man I was liv-

ing with years ago, and he

ordered lamb, and I had to go into the bathroom and start crying because I just couldn't believe I was involved with someone who could eat lamb.

Natalie Merchant
Issue 652 · March 18th, 1993

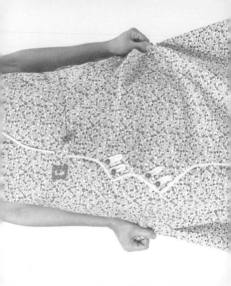

I do believe relationships can last. I see these old people who are together in their eighties, holding hands. I think that's really neat. I think that's probably one of the hardest things to do in the world, to be a human being, maintain a relationship, be a decent person.

Billy Joel

ISSUE 486 · November 6th, 1986

I regret relationships that I got into where I didn't have my armor on. But if it wasn't for these things, I would never have had to ask myself why I did these things, why I attracted these people, why I couldn't protect myself emotionally. Now I have my armor as a result of

Sinéad O'Connor

Issue 642 • October 29th, 1992

not having
had it.

My life in the last six years has been a Disney film and now I have to have a person in my life.

Elton John

ISSUE 223 · October 7th, 1976

Could I bring another man into all of this? I don't intend to spend the rest of my life alone, but in this state of mind, it would be very unfair to any man who gets involved with me. Because I am still very involved.

Yoko Ono

ISSUE 353 · October 1st, 1981

Somebody once said that being **married** is about having a best friend. . . . Like I'm walking down the street with my **best friend** and going, "Look at the way that stocking seam goes up that chick's legs." . . . I might want to in another lifetime, but I'm not going to now because **I love my wife**.

Steven Tyler

(Aerosmith)
ISSUE 694 · November 3rd, 1994

With relationships, how do you position yourself in relation to other people? It's a fine line sometimes, trying to hold on to yourself and your own identity and either being lured into having other people define them for you or having the things around you define them for you.

Tracy Chapman

ISSUE 529 · June 30th, 1988

I MENTIONED ONE MOR
NING TO JAMES [TAYLO
R] IN LONDON THAT I
THOUGHT WE SHOULD
GET MARRIED, AND JAM
ES WAS KIND OF HESIT
ANT IN HIS RESPONSE.
HE SAID, "OH WELL, THER
E'S REALLY NO REASO
N TO GET MARRIED. WE
LOVE EACH OTHER, A
ND WE'VE BEEN LIVING
TOGETHER." AND THEN

LATER ON IN THE AFTERNOON, JAMES SAID, "YOU KNOW I'VE BEEN THINKING ABOUT IT, AND MAYBE WE SHOULD GET MARRIED." I SAID, "WELL, WHAT'S HAPPENED BETWEEN THIS MORNING AND THIS AFTERNOON?" HE SAID, "THIS AFTERNOON IT WAS MY IDEA." CARLY SIMON ISSUE 125 · JULY 4TH, 1973

I think the ultimate lover will be like being alone. It will be so comfortable, I won't have a problem sleeping or feel I have to entertain them or worry about them or worry about them understanding me. I think I'll know her when I see her. I hope.

k.d. lang

ISSUE 662 · August 5th, 1993

With relation- ships, for me, it's always a case of a work in progress.

Peter Gabriel

ISSUE 492 · January 29th, 1987

I'M NOT REALLY SURE THAT I'M LOOKING FOR COMFORT OR A STEADY RELATIONSHIP. I JUST LIKE THE COMPANY OF BEAUTIFUL WOMEN. I HAVE A WEAKNESS IN THAT DEPARTMENT. AND I SUPPOSE BECAUSE I AM FAIRLY WELL OFF AND A FAMOUS MUSICIAN, I'M UP FOR GRABS. AND THAT MAKES ME AN ELIGIBLE BACHELOR IN THE PRESS.

ISSUE 615 · October 17th, 1991

I can't really come to terms with what marriage means, especially nowadays. The fact that you can be divorced sort of nullifies the whole spirit of marriage. And I guess I don't like what I see in it when I look at other people. I don't wanna be like them.

Chrissie Hynde

(the Pretenders)
ISSUE 420 · April 26th, 1984

When you get into what you want in your life and how much of a certain thing you want—letting someone in your life is a personal thing. That doesn't say that in my life I haven't hung out. I'd be lying to say that I didn't. But you can only really live a life with real relationships.

Stevie Wonder

ISSUE 471 · April 10th, 1986

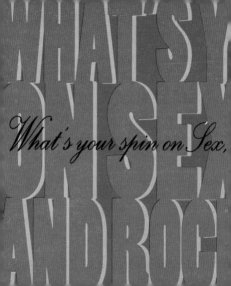

What's your spin on Sex,

Love and Rock & Roll?

Ya know, people say to me, "Aren't you afraid of becoming a sex object?". . . Well, I find that very exciting. I think sex is one of the five highest sensations one can experience.

Patti Smith

ISSUE 270 · July 27th, 1978

The birth of rock & roll coincided with my adolescence, my coming into awareness. It was a real turn-on, although at the time I could never allow myself to rationally fantasize about ever doing it myself.

Jim Morrison

(the Doors)

ISSUE 38 · July 26th, 1969

My sex life is absolutely the centerpiece of everything that's ever written about me and I probably have a lot less sex than other people — that's the final irony of it all.

Madonna · ISSUE 692 · October 6th, 1994

as corny as it sounds, my life has been consumed by rock music. I just loved it right from the beginning.

Tom Petty

ISSUE 610 · August 8th, 1991

It's the music that keeps me alive, and my relationships with my friends, and my attachment to the people and the places I've known. That's my lifeblood.

Bruce Springsteen

ISSUE 436 · December 6th, 1984

The Beatles used to say, "We won't be rock & rollin' when we're forty," but I still love it.

Paul McCartney

ISSUE 482 · September 11th, 1986

Rock & roll to me is communication. I don't just
mean communication of ideas, but
communication of feelings.

The Edge

(U2)
ISSUE 521 · March 10th, 1988

You see

isn't just fire and heat,

it's natural beauty.

Doing what comes naturally.

It's letting go, giving and getting

what you need.

ISSUE 665
September 16th, 1993

Unrequited love is a subject very near and dear to my heart. I have a whole well of inspiration when it comes to that.

Bette Midler

ISSUE 306 · December 13th, 1979

When you study **the man** and **the woman,** you can get a great sort of **command of emotion** with your poetry.

Donovan

ISSUE 1 · November 9th, 1967

Most songs are basically like love songs, and I don't feel like I'm exactly the most romantic person in the world. So **I can only do so many love songs** without feeling like an idiot.

Jerry Garcia

ISSUE 616 · October 31st, 1991

The music always came first. I think we wanted it that way. I mean, it would have been very nice—we wanted to have relationships with girls and have the band, too. But it just didn't seem possible. We were wedded to the muse or that vision—whatever it was and however murky it might have been.

Don Henley

(the Eagles)
ISSUE 587 · September 20th, 1990

Very few of my albums are love songs to anyone. Music is so big, man, it just takes up a lot of room. I've dedicated my life to my music so far. And every time I've let it slip and gotten somewhere else, it's showed. Music lasts . . . a lot longer than relationships do.

Neil Young

ISSUE 193 · August 14th, 1975

I know a lot of guys from the old days who wouldn't get married because it might affect their careers. The old management thing—"You can't get married, all your fans are going to desert you." So the guy doesn't get married. But the thing is, in a couple of years, his career is over anyway. And he didn't get married, and he went and blew it.

Paul McCartney

ISSUE 153 · January 31st, 1974

It can really eat into a relationship when you are involved with someone you work with and the world is not reinforcing your work together.

Bonnie Raitt

ISSUE 577 · May 3rd, 1990

What I feel about music now is that I love God, I always will love God, and I feel that I am a messenger for him. To me, rock & roll music is the only way I know how to make a living. I'm making people joyful, and I still spread my love for God. So I'm still the person that God has placed, but the music is my job.

Little Richard

ISSUE 576 · April 19th, 1990

I was active and physically doing the things that were sexual when I was younger. There was one side of me that was crazy and deviant, doing things ahead of my time, and another side that was very held back, wanting to remain virginal for the sake of being the good white Catholic girl.

Alanis Morissette

ISSUE 720 · November 2nd, 1995

To actually

have sex

when you are

in love

is the best way.

Tina Turner

ISSUE 485 · October 23rd, 1986

I was in a disco when I had my first kiss, and it was a disgusting experience, saliva everywhere. Probably Sylvester was on. You remember the music that was around when important things were happening in your life. I still like Sylvester to this day.

Lisa Stansfield

ISSUE 582/583 · July 12th-26th, 1990

I'm pretty amazed by my own sexuality. I'm not completely in touch with it, but it runs through everything I do.

Tanya Donelly

(Belly)

ISSUE 649 · February 4th, 1993

I love feeling deeply sexual and don't mind letting the world know. For me, sex has become a celebration, a joyful part of the creative process.

Janet Jackson

ISSUE 665 · September 16th, 1993

The way I was reared, the role model
for women was the Virgin Mary,
the sexless thing. Responsible girls
were virgins until they were married.
I didn't understand why I couldn't
just merge with someone and have a
wonderful time and not have to stay
with them forever.

Tori Amos

ISSUE 685 · June 30th, 1994

We sort of stand for everybody's

I'd call it humanistic, too. It's the

sexuality, not just freaks'. We're

power and strength of the male side

not women dominating men or the

of the rock scene along with the

other w around — sexual fan-

more delicate and appealing female

tasy that we give onstage is a very

talents on the acoustic music — in

natural one. Ann Wilson (Heart)

the soul Nancy Wilson (Heart)

ISSUE 244 • July 28th, 1977

Issue 244 • July 28th, 1977

I don't think our sexuality is belligerent; it's more a free-flowing musical display. And that's only one small part of who we are. If you made a list of every song that we've ever written, maybe 10 percent would be sexually dominated.

Anthony Kiedis

(Red Hot Chili Peppers)
ISSUE 679 · April 7th, 1994

I've felt often in our relationship that I've been addicted to James [Taylor] and I have a dependency upon him that's almost like a drug I couldn't do without. Maybe that's what addiction is all about.

Carly Simon

ISSUE 125 · January 4th, 1973

YOUR
BAND
YOUR
and
FANS?

It's not easy
group. It's li
without sex.
LUBRICANT
is music.

to be in a

ke marriage

The only

we have

Sting

(referring to the Police)
ISSUE 403 · September 1st, 1983

When I'm onstage, I am **in love with everyone** on that stage. Whatever may happen outside of it is petty by comparison.

Tina Weymouth

(Talking Heads)
ISSUE 491 · January 15th, 1987

Sometimes everybody in the band comes over, and we have very long talks. I think they love me so much, and I love them so much, that if they came over all the time I wouldn't be able to be to them what I am, and they wouldn't be able to do for me what they do. I think we all need our individual spaces, and when we come together with what we've concocted in our heads, it's cool.

Prince

ISSUE 456 · September 12th, 1985

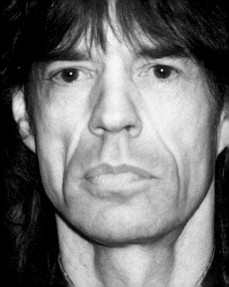

WE'RE VERY CLOSE, AND
WE ALWAYS HAVE BEEN.
[KEITH RICHARDS] WAS
BORN MY BROTHER BY
ACCIDENT BY DIFFER-
ENT PARENTS.

Mick Jagger
(the Rolling Stones)
ISSUE 268 · June 29th, 1978

We tend to come together only when there's work. It really is like Christmas with the family; you get on all right, but you know you wouldn't be able to stand it if they were living with you for a month. And I wouldn't! I wouldn't be able to stand to live with Keith or Mick, and I'm sure they couldn't stand it either.

Bill Wyman

(the Rolling Stones)
ISSUE 324 · August 21st, 1980

We're like
BROTHERS
you know?
we LOVE each
other and we
HATE
each other
NEIL YOUNG
(REFERRING TO
STEPHEN STILLS)
Issue 52/June 2nd, 1988

The last thing I want to do is sleep with a fan. Because k.d. lang the performer is so much cooler than me. Not that there's really a difference, but as a lover, I'm not as self-assured and cocky and invincible as she is.

k.d. lang

ISSUE 662 · August 5th, 1993

I wanted the real me to be appreciated, not the performing me. I didn't particularly want to be loved for the way I played the guitar. The way I played guitar was part of my angry side, my rebellious side. What my audience loved me most for was something that was only a small part of me.

Pete Townshend

ISSUE 512 · November 5th-December 10th, 1987

girl-type screams are silly. When you get a guy that screams, an appreciative-type yell, encouragement, that can kind of turn you on when you're performing.

Rod Stewart

ISSUE 73 · December 24th, 1970

Simon and Garfunkel had a peculiar type of groupie. We had the poetic groupies. The girls that followed us around weren't necessarily looking to sleep with us as much as they were looking to read their poetry or discuss literature or play their own songs.

Paul Simon

ISSUE 113 · July 20th, 1972

If some people had their way, they'd just want me to weep and suffer for them for the rest of my life, because people live vicariously through their artists. And I had that grand theme for a long time: Where is my mate? Where is my mate? Where is my mate? I got rid of that one.

Joni Mitchell

ISSUE 605 · May 30th, 1991

I do feel I can communicate to large groups of people, but they have to know what they're getting, and I have to know what I'm giving. It's quality, not quantity.

Van Morrison

ISSUE 62 · July 9th, 1970

Of course, you get exhausted. You want to pass out. I came close a couple of times. But you're filled with something, that feedback that comes from the audience. You feel so strong that if somebody shot you with a gun you could keep going.

Clarence Clemons

(the E Street Band)
ISSUE 468 · February 27th, 1986

Being
onstage is magic.
There's nothing like it.
You feel the energy of
everybody who's out
there. You feel it all
over your body.

Michael Jackson

ISSUE 389 · FEBRUARY 17TH, 1983

I just dig audiences. That to me is the most worthwhile thing about this whole business. Just people coming to have a good time and letting me sing for them. . . . Because, man, when I look out at an audience, all I see are beautiful people.

Stevie Wonder

ISSUE 189 · June 19th, 1975

orget the press—just being a partner of somebody who's very, very famous, it's hard to keep your center and your personality intact.

Patti Scialfa

(the E Street Band)
ISSUE 667 · October 14th, 1993

PHOTO CREDITS LAURA LEVINE: *David Bowie, Elvis Costello, Boy George, Chrissie Hynde, Natalie Merchant, Sinéad O'Connor* · GUZMAN/WARNER BROS.: *k. d. lang* · WARNER BROS.: *Bonnie Raitt* · ARCHIVE PHOTOS/POP-PERFOTO: *Madonna* · PATRICK DEMARCHELIER ©1995 BLACK DOLL, INC.: *Janet Jackson* · CINDY PALMANO/AT-LANTIC: *Tori Amos* · GENE SHAW/STAR FILE: *Mick Jagger* **ILLUSTRATION CREDITS** MARGIE GREVE: *Pete Townshend and Eric Clapton* · LAURA LEVINE: *True Love*

This book has been bound using handcraft methods, and is Smyth-sewn to ensure durability · Cover design by Gail Anderson · Interior design by Frances J. Soo Ping Chow · Edited by Mary McGuire · The text was set in Kemerley, HTF Ziggurat, Palace Script and Poplar

-265